TRAPS WITHIN THE TRIALS

WALKING IN TRIUMPH

HENRY M. D. RICHARDS

WESTBOW
PRESS®
A DIVISION OF THOMAS NELSON
& ZONDERVAN

WestBow Press books may be ordered through booksellers or by contacting:

WestBow Press
A Division of Thomas Nelson & Zondervan
1663 Liberty Drive
Bloomington, IN 47403
www.westbowpress.com
844-714-3454

Scripture quotations taken from The Holy Bible, New International
Version® NIV® Copyright © 1973 1978 1984 2011 by Biblica, Inc.
TM. Used by permission. All rights reserved worldwide.

ISBN: 978-1-6642-4228-9 (sc)
ISBN: 978-1-6642-4227-2 (e)

Print information available on the last page.

WestBow Press rev. date: 08/23/2021

CONTENTS

PREFACE

By nature, we human beings are very impatient. As a result, we understand that our human nature often wars against our spiritual nature because of our immaturity which clouds our ability to see things God's way. Thus God allows us to go through trials that are the used as teaching moments and building blocks for the maturing Believer. God has to break the old prideful immature nature and allow patience and obedience to be developed in us along with other needed characteristics for our purpose. In other words He helps us mature. In this book, I have tried to explain that patience and obedience are key tools to overcoming the temptations, trials, and traps we will undoubtedly encounter in life.

I desire that all Christians, young Christians and youth Christians especially, will be better able to recognize some of the more common traps as a result of reading this book.

However bad a situation seems to be, I encourage you to share it with God. He is our Jehovah Shammah (ever-present). You can rest assured that He is always there, ready to listen, and willing to bring you out in victory!

I wrote this book to help you realize that trials are God's classroom for you. However, in every classroom, they are distractions that can stop you from passing the class. These distractions can also be referred to as traps.

Be aware, alert, and a success. It's God's plan for your life.

ACKNOWLEDGMENTS

To my pastor, brother, friend, and laborer in the Lord, Terry W. Richards, I want to thank you for coming beside me in my chaotic time and walking through my restoration and stability process. You held me accountable and advised me in every decision, and kept reminding me that it would all work out for my best.

To my family Alfred and Nadia, Sonia and Steve, Elon and Michelle and last, but not least the administrators Diana and Stephen. Thank you for the rock-solid support in all that I do and for keeping Mum's values and instilled teachings of "family must always be family no matter what." Your never-ending encouragement and love are rocks in my life.

To my precious daughters, Gabby and Klynisha. You make me strive to be an example and measuring stick for you as a Christian but most of all, a man. Thank you for your irreplaceable love, and being your dad is a blessing and an honor.

To Mums, Mrs. Janet Connolly, if it's one thing I can say is that from the moment your realized what was in me you never stopped encouraging or believing. Your encouragement to publish this book so long ago has not been in vain and is coming to a reality. Bless you and don't stop doing what God has called you to do. It's your season to step out.

To Shakira, my friend, and all-in believer in what God has deposited in me. Thank you for insisting that I not leave this book filed away and for your persistence in encouraging me to sow my seed. Thank you for giving me that nudge and believing in this book but most of all God's call on my life.

To my Dad, who could not give me riches or fame but gave me the best and most important thing a parent can give their child, an introduction to knowing Christ as my Savior. Thank you for laying down the law that no matter where we went or how late we returned home, Sunday morning was church and we had to be there. You ensured that our household was aware of, loved, and served God.

To Mummy, the Lady, the Loved, the Legend. I am forever indebted to you, and words cannot do it justice. I'll say thank you for lifting me before God every single day of my life and asking God to keep His hands on my life. There was never a time when you turned your back, even when I was stubborn and thought I knew it all. You always showed me love, and even if a stiff rebuke accompanied it, you never withheld either because you understood to avoid spoiling the child you cannot spare the rod. As Terry and I would constantly talk about the fact that you did not go to university nor were you any profound minister but the principles you lived and taught us could only be taught to you directly from God. Flesh and blood dint not reveal them to you but only God. I'm proud to be called "Mummy's Second Last" and I love and miss you.

ABOUT THE AUTHOR

Minister Henry Richards is a Barbadian Minister of the Gate Keepers International Ministries. Minister Henry serves as an assistant to Pastor Terry W. Richards, who founded the ministry in 2019 under God's guidance. Pastor Richards established the ministry to focus on "the healing and restoration of the broken and the maturation of God's people to prepare them to live out their purposes."

Minister Henry Richards is driven to see the body of Christ, especially the next generation, freed from the spirit of ignorance through religiosity and traditions. He believes in cutting-edge revelations and teachings that motivate the Believer to be mobilized and pursue God authentically and passionately.

His teachings and ministry are said to motivate and inspire the new generation to live out their Christianity aloud but in alignment with the revelation of who God is. He's driven by "Purpose over Pleasure." He hopes that when his life's journey is over, everyone who came in contact with his ministry would have been infected by the desire to fulfill their purpose. He also hopes that they would not have been deceived by the pleasures of satisfaction offered by this world.

Minister Henry Richards is 47 years old and has been in the faith since the age of 16. He is the 5th child of his beloved parents Alfred and Joycelyn Richards, who have gone home to be with the Lord. His siblings, Diana Leacock, Elon Richards, Terry Richards, Sonia Richards-Humphrey, and Alfred Junior Richards, are all walking in the faith. Their late mother would say they are proof that prayer works in keeping them all in the House of God. He is the father of a biological daughter, Gabrielle Richards, and the proud stepdad of his ex-wife's daughter, Klynisha Connolly.

Minister Richards grew up in the local First Baptist Church on Constitution Road, St. Michael, Barbados. There his Christian journey began, along with developing his appetite for the word of God. He loves the Lord, and the study and revelation of the Word both excite and consume him. He believes that the Word of God is the answer to any and everything in life. He is most excited when he sees the spiritual scales falling off a listener's eyes—seeing their faces illuminated.

INTRODUCTION

No Christian wants to sin or desires to live in sin. Still, because human beings are spirit beings housed in earthly bodies, we are in a constant battle between walking in the ways of God and walking after the desires of the flesh.

Whether young or old, childlike or mature in your Christian walk with God, we all wrestle with the flesh's desires. These desires oppose us as we seek to live in alignment with God's principles, expectations, and purpose for our lives. This battle never ends.

Why are these struggles so crucial for believers to win? For starters, if we don't overcome, we will be overwhelmed by the enemy (the devil) and his schemes to steal, kill and destroy us. We are guaranteed to experience **trials** that God will use to equip us for the battlefield of life. As we overcome them, we will move one step closer to being transformed to the likeness of Christ in being a Son and accomplishing our predestined purpose. Through overcoming these trials, each of us can become the sons God created us to be.

How we handle these challenges also determines our effectiveness in our Christian walk. We are called by God and taken through a process of transformation. This process then allows us to reform our circles, communities, nations, and, ultimately, the whole creation. Thus, we really cannot afford to fall victim to the enemy's devices.

In Romans 7:14-20, Paul states that as long as we are alive in the flesh, the desire to carry out the Lord's ways will be challenged by our sinful nature, which is fueled by sin. We will constantly grapple with the choice of walking in God's ways instead of gratifying the flesh. We can only win this battle if we follow the directions written in God's word. We have to choose Him over everything else, one decision at a time.

We know that God's law is spiritual but I am unspiritual (A creature of flesh) having being sold into slavery under the control of sin. For I do not understand my own actions. I do not practice or accomplish what I wish, but I do the very thing that I hate, which my spiritual mind condemns. And if I habitually do what is contrary to my desire, I agree the law of the world is good. However, it is no longer I myself who do the deeds, but it is the sin that has possession of me. For I know that nothing good lives within me, that is, in my sinful nature (flesh). For I have the desire to do what is right, but I cannot carry it out. For I fail to practice the good deeds I desire to do, but the evil deed that I do not desire to do I keep doing. Now if I do what I do not desire to do, it is no longer I who do it but it is the sinful nature that possesses me that does it. **Romans 7:14-20**

As a young Christian man, I found this war to be brutal. At times it was as if I was being consumed and controlled by my fleshly desires. These desires then caused me to stumble from the path of righteousness as if I was being held hostage by the devil.

At some point in every Christian's life, these seemingly uncontrollable sinful desires will arise, especially young persons. Of course, you can cry out earnestly to God for strength while also wrestling in your understanding. You can find yourselves seeking desperately to understand how you can be so vulnerable. Yet, at other times you can feel so immovable and grounded in God, simply by the everyday choices you make in each circumstance and situation.

In all areas of our lives, we can experience situations that overwhelm us and cause us to stumble or even fall. These situations often arise at times when we are seeking to advance to another level of living. Whether it is in a job, school, finances, or marriage, these situations challenge our stability and our comfort. They can push us to the point of total confusion and insecurity.

"But every person is tempted when he is drawn away, enticed and baited by his own evil desires/lust/passions. Then the evil desire, when it is conceived, gives birth to sin, and sin, when it is fully matured, brings forth death." (James 1 vs.14-15)

The book of James refers to these testing situations as Trials. In contrast, in the book of 1 Corinthians, Paul explains what they are and differentiates between a Trial and a Temptation.

This book will more closely study James' and Paul's explanations by taking an in-depth look at the spiritual significance of trials and temptations. It will also discuss how we can effectively guard against traps and remain in alignment with God's purpose for our lives as we walk effectively in our righteousness.

1

TRIALS VS. TEMPTATIONS

We have just highlighted one of the enemy's most effective lies to the Christian community. Actually, to all humanity: Trials, not Temptations, are solely created to draw us closer to and not push us further from God. There are similarities but also significant differences deserving of closer study. The two are not entirely separate, as there are some interesting relationships between the two.

Let us first re-establish that a Trial is not the same as Temptation. We should also accept that many temptations arise within trials. As we discussed in the previous chapter, when we are being tried, it means that God has placed us in the circumstances to teach us how to draw on Him more. In contrast, temptations are situations that the devil has devised to cause us to sin. These temptations are usually geared towards areas in your life where you may be weak, struggling or worse, think you are too strong to fall in. The enemy creates these moments of temptation to distract us from God's will and complicate our walk. Satan knows if we only succumb to the temptation, our efforts at living righteous will be undermined, and he will have succeeded in destroying our testimony.

In James 1:13-14, we are told: "*Let no man say when he is tempted, I am tempted by God; for God is incapable of being tempted by what is evil and He Himself tempts no one. But everyone is tempted when he is drawn away, enticed and baited by his own evil desires, lust, and passions."* Here we can see the contrast between our temptations and trials **and** the connection between temptations and lust.

We should never forget that the enemy is *always* seeking to lie, cheat and destroy. What is essential to understand is how the devil works within our trials' framework and exploits them to create temptation. This temptation then appears to offer a route of escape from the difficulties of the trial.

For example, how do you overcome a trial where you are seeking God's grace and guidance on controlling youthful lust? Especially when decide to diligently apply His principles revealed from His Word to keep your flesh in subjection because you earnestly want to live purely and righteously for God? You overcome the trial by acknowledging that within the trial, your fleshly desires may still be there. However, by consciously stifling the flesh, you enable the spiritual being to conquer and reign.

When we endure and overcome each trial, our relationship with God goes to a deeper level of intimacy, and our lives continue to be very fulfilling. Each growth spurt enables the opportunity to see significant displays of the Fruits of the Spirit.

TRIALS

Trials are simply scenarios of life that God uses in our maturation process.

The book of James helps us to see these trials as opportunities to develop our faith and perseverance where he states:

"Consider it a pure joy, my brothers, whenever you face trials of many kinds, (3) because you know that the testing of your faith develops perseverance. (4) Perseverance must finish its work so that you may be mature and complete, not lacking anything. (12) Blessed is the man who perseveres under trial, because when he has stood the test, he will receive the crown of life that God has promised to those who love Him." James 1: 2-4, 12

We all feel like there is something or someone out to get us by pushing all the right buttons to frustrate us at some point in time. In response, we become relaxed and stop being vigilant. Before we know it, we have put down our sword and became a civilian in the heat of the battle between righteousness and sinfulness. We feel propelled to divert from our predestined calling by God to appease our fleshly cravings. At these times, our love and desire to please God and fulfill His call in our lives should motivate us to persevere and not find ourselves sidelined and defeated.

James advises us to consider it a "Pure Joy" when we face different trials, assuring us that the testing of our faith develops perseverance. The problem with considering trials as "Pure Joy" usually comes when we are in the midst of the trial. We can soon be caught up with the sound of the storm rather than focusing on where we are heading if we're not alert. We will stay the course and operate more effectively if we understand why we are going through the storm. Understanding is preferred rather than focusing on how big the storm is and what disaster it can cause.

These trials always create an environment for a revelation of our purpose in life while giving us a sense of meaning. They present stepping stones to take us to a higher level of righteous living. They also provide solutions and victories over struggles in our walk and bring us to the revelation of God's perfect will. Going through trials should be seen as a process that serves to bring us closer to His Likeness. This process is all wrapped up in "Knowing Him better" and ultimately knowing who we truly are.

Every trial has a purpose in God's plan of refinement for us, but we need to accept and trust the work He is perfectly doing in us. Wisdom is only acquired through revering and fearing God [Proverbs 9:10]. We need it to live and make it through our trials effectively. Wisdom is revealed when we spend more time in God's Word, learning the desires of His heart. We then apply the Principles of the Kingdom to our lives through the government of the Holy Spirit.

As we persevere through each trial, God blesses us for our faith in Him. In addition, we acquire greater wisdom and are more mature and refined in our walk with Him.

We must remember that trials should not be allowed to distract us from pursuing or serving God. Instead, they should help bring us into a closer relationship with Him as we seek to draw from the wisdom that will comfort, strengthen and cause more attentiveness to Him. Trials serve to build character and increase our passion and determination to be even more faithful to God because of His overwhelming faithfulness to us.

TEMPTATIONS

Whereas trials are allowed and used by God, temptations are moments where the devil appeals to our cravings for fleshly satisfaction. He gets us to sin [disobey God's word] and fall in our Christian walk. Never negate the part we play at this moment because if we never craved it, it would not tempt us. These situations are schemed by the devil and focus on our weaknesses and proclivities (James 1 vs. 13-14). We all have proclivities that influence our decision-making and force us to either walk in righteousness or fall for the lust of our flesh. However, we need to know that these temptations are strategically and uniquely manufactured within the framework of God's allowed trials for our refinement.

The devil is much more intelligent than Christians give Him credit for. If we go back to the Garden of Eden in the account of the fall of man, the devil chose to use a snake that was deemed the most crafty of all animals created. He is the master of counterfeits and schemes, and he thrives on copying all of God's allowed trials for our growth and wholeness. Within God's trial-created situations, the devil devises a counterfeit simulation specially catered to our lusts to trip us up.

Never be ignorant or be caught unawares. The devil will always seek to lure us into sin because he is very aware of our weaknesses. If you were the devil and wanted to trick and trap Christians, wouldn't you think the best way would be to imitate everything that could catch Christians who were not vigilant? If I were the devil, I would. I would spend significant time mimicking the great Creator and simulating situations that camouflaged their real purpose. My sole goal would be to cripple and derail you from your journey.

Most assuredly, God does not set us up in temptations that can lead to our demise. Why would God tempt us? When you sin, it causes separation between Him and us because sin creates that wedge between us. Would a God that loves and desires the best for us set us up to fail? Never!

God orchestrates all our trials to give us strength, teach us principles and equip us with wisdom and authority to have dominion over sin. Remember, this is the same God that gave His Son for humanity to save us from the bondage of sin and its consequence of death. God loves us too much to trick us into separation from Him through sin. Not only does He love us so much, but He hates sin even more. Jesus (His only Son) painfully bore our sins and carried them all to the grave in His death so that we could be free from all life's bondages. Wouldn't the entire act of the gruesome crucifixion be all in vain? Wouldn't Jesus's suffering and disgrace be a mockery? Would God give His Son to be abused and slain by man and then turn around and slap Him in the face by tricking us into what hinders us from intimacy with Him? Wouldn't this cause Jesus great pain and sadness? I surely do not think God would do that!

There is no temptation that is not common to man, but God always gives an escape (1 Corinthians 10:13). God, who is true love, will never save you and then trap you in the bondage of sin, especially when He plans to prosper you and give you hope and a future He predestined for you. God is more committed to you becoming your best you than even you are.

2

MANEUVERING THE TRAPS

In Psalms 119, David establishes the importance of following the Word as the key to righteous and victorious living. This chapter will reveal a five-part formula we need to apply to our lives to maneuver the enemy's traps successfully. We must bring ourselves to:

1. Admitting dependency on God and repentance
2. Dedication to studying the Word
3. Prayer
4. Walking in tune with the spirit
5. Obedience

ADMITTANCE & REPENTANCE

We all need to start by repenting for our disobedience to God's word and admit that we are helpless without Him. We need to acknowledge that without His supreme wisdom, revealed to us through the Holy Spirit; we will be constantly deceived and trapped by the enemy. Worst yet, we will also be caught in a constant struggle to overcome sin. The devil has repeatedly abused us in our lives because of our weaknesses, inadequacies, and lust which leaves us in disarray and disappointment. We are no match for the devil, and Paul reminds us in *Ephesians 6:12-17* that our struggles are not in the flesh but the spirit. Therefore, we need to put on our spiritual armor if we are to even have a chance at winning.

Preparation is only possible through sincere admittance that we are failures in ourselves and confess our dependence on God. Admitting such dependence is humbling, which is the posture God always wants us to be in. Even David accepted he had fleshly limitations and always needed God's help to keep from sinning daily. David asks in **Psalms 119:9**, *"How can a man keep his way pure"* and moves on to answer, *"By living according to the Word."* As simple as this sounds, it is precisely the formula for living a life that keeps us in the will of God and away from the constant abuse and traps the devil has for us. Even Jesus had to apply this principle by daily seeking the Will of the Father.

Acts of Admittance and Repentance are acts of humility, and it is only by humility that God's heart is remotely moved.

Once we understand this, we will always be able to capture God's heart and be even more overwhelmed by His response and presence. If humility captures God's heart, what would it be like to live in total humility and awe of God? Can you imagine the impact and authority we would walk in?

STUDYING THE WORD

The Word of God will always serve as a guide for us by revealing His ways and expectations, which gives us the passion for knowing Him better. To know God better is to understand His heart, and understanding His heart inspires us to accomplish His predestined purpose for our lives. God's word reveals God! It reveals His will for our lives and presents principles that will keep us on the "paths of righteousness," which He has already laid out for us. As we get to know God better, our steps become more focused and precise because our minds are being renewed.

Most importantly, we are developing a lifestyle that's refined in the likeness of a son. When we know Him, our hearts become more passionate about Him and His ways. We acquire joy in and about Him that arouses desires to always be in His presence and please Him. In John 14:15, Christ tells us if you love God, then please Him by obeying His commands. When we have an insatiable love for Jesus, our attitude is more Christ-like, and we hunger after what He wants.

We must understand that such an attitude and posture will not exclude us from the devil's schemes. Instead, it sharpens and empowers us to handle them more effectively and efficiently. When we seek guidance in the word of God, we are better equipped to skillfully maneuver through any situation orchestrated by the devil to break us. Hence, David could boldly declare the need to give God governance over his life and seek after His heart; because it is the only way to live righteously.

To get even more profound: The more time we spend in God's Word, the more we develop our faith, and the more we unleash the true you that His word empowers.

Faith is a fruit of God's word, so no word, no faith, and if you have no faith, you cannot please God. You cannot get anything from the Kingdom, and you definitely will not have any power to function in the authority you need.

Firstly, Romans 10:17 tells us that faith comes from hearing and believing the word of God. Simply put, if we are to live by faith as God expects, then we cannot stay away from His word and expect to walk in faith. Faith is a byproduct of God's word, so no word, no faith, and if you have no faith, you cannot please God. You cannot get anything from the Kingdom, and you definitely will not have any power to function in the authority you need. Faith is the Kingdom's currency, so anything you want to access depends on the potency of faith you have. If you want faith, then meditate on God's word, and you'll see how much more prepared you will be, not just to recognize the traps but to overcome them.

Secondly, the source of our power in our lives is bound up in the Word, and it is brought to life in us through the Holy Spirit. The Holy Spirit is the "Dunamis" power of God for us, but it cannot work in and through us if there's no word in us.

Hebrews 4:12 tells us that sin targets three areas in our lives, and the Word must get deep inside of us to address:

- Our soul and spirit deal with our sinful nature.
- The bone and marrow that houses our hereditary curses and proclivities that have us imprisoned
- Our thoughts and attitudes that house our present and conscious daily desires that contradict God's thoughts and desires for us.

Grasping this, you can understand why David tells us in Psalms 119:9 that the only way we can cleanse and change our ways is through the Word of God. Nothing else can get into the core of man and redefine him. Anything else will be superficial and only dampens or camouflages that issue. When you face a trial or, even worse, a trap, you'll see that old nature erupt at the surface.

"For the word of God is living and active and full of power [making it operative, energizing, and effective]. It is sharper than any two-edged sword, penetrating as far as the division of the soul and spirit [the completeness of a person], and of both joints and marrow [the deepest parts of our nature], exposing and judging the very thoughts and intentions of the heart." Hebrews 4:12

PRAYER

Prayer is our direct line of communication with God that creates an open heaven for God to operate in our lives or in the circumstance we are petitioning about. Prayer gives God legal freedom to act on our behalf. It is not just when we list every request we can think of and every distress we experience. Rather, it is a time when we can sincerely ask God for His direction and desires, but most of all, give Him the chance to influence earth with heaven.

Prayer empowers us to handle life in the authority we are given in Christ by positioning us to be used by God as He desires.

Prayer should be a time of building our spirit by glorifying God and thanking Him for His great mercies and revelations that are new and accurate each day. Not to mention a time when we surrender our pride of life and humble ourselves before the King of kings. When we pray thankfully and are full of praise, we grab God's heart and attention, and we access the power and authority that He has made available to us. Yes, prayer does empower us to handle life in the authority we are given in Christ by positioning us to be used by God as He desires. We are empowered as we recognize and praise God for the power and love that He so readily avails to us through His Son.

While on earth, Jesus prayed continually on many occasions for the power of the Lord to reside in Him to accomplish the Father's will. Christ was always praying for the accomplishment of the Father's will. Furthermore, if you were to investigate the scriptures, you would see Christ constantly praying before all those fantastic and incredible miracles.

The Father's will for our lives can only be accomplished if we know what it is. Like **Matthew 7:7** assures us: *"Ask and it shall be given, seek and we will find, knock and it will be opened for us."* Christians are called to do His will, to serve and praise Him, while accomplishing that purpose He has called us to as part of the work of the Christian body. This work is where we utilize the talents and gifts we are all blessed with to serve both the unbelievers and believers. Remember our great commission in Matthew 28:19 compels us to **"Go *and make disciples of all nations…."***

Prayer keeps us in a posture of humility to exalt God's will over our will and facilitate our maturation. It gives guidance to make the right decisions in alignment with God's heart. Additionally, it empowers us with authority to be more than conquerors in our traps. Often, we have preset outcomes and plans for situations and lives that are not necessarily what God has lined up for us. Therefore, we need to acknowledge His plans and submit to the process of their unfolding. This process will also endow you with the authority to crush and control your flesh that wars against God.

Paul always faced trials but still significantly impacted others as an Apostle because he continually sought God in prayer and His heart and desires for his life. Paul never withdrew from doing what God commissioned him to do. Even when Paul was under house arrest, he still fulfilled his purpose and transformed lives up to this day. Trials aren't meant to break you. Instead, they can propel you into a deeper intimacy that results in a more mature and impactful disciple of Christ.

Another man after God's heart was David, who continually sought God in prayer. Often, David was either in prayer for forgiveness of his sin, asking for guidance, or seeking deliverance from his enemies. I also realize that David was constant in prayer, declaring and decreeing the destiny of God's people and the destruction of all those after us. We, too, need this reliance on prayer because we always need deliverance from the enemy. And, of course, each of us needs continual guidance in the "Pathway of Righteousness."

Because we know that God is always with us, we should realize that He also desires conversations. He wants to share His heart with us and join forces to see His Kingdom come and His will done. Therefore, when you pray, wait a while and spend time listening. Give God a chance to respond, and you'll see that your prayers will be powerful and effective.

IN TUNE WITH THE SPIRIT

"And I will ask the Father, and he will give you another advocate to help you and be with you forever— the Spirit of truth. The world cannot accept him, because it neither sees him nor knows him. But you know him, for he lives with you and will be in you." John 14:16-17

To be remotely successful in our Christian journey, we need to submit ourselves to the government and leadership of the Holy Spirit. We must let Him guide us in the ways of the Father, or else we will find ourselves constantly in situations and scenarios that can be pretty troubling.

The truth is that everything in the world is not wrong or even destructive, but how you pursue or aspire for it could destroy you. Every decision you make on your own will not always be wrong for you, but the question you should ask yourself is; is it beneficial and getting you where you want to go?

Paul tells us that everything is permissible but isn't always profitable. Determining what is profitable therefore is premised on your goal and, most importantly, whose will you are trying to fulfill. Suppose it's God's will and not yours. In that case, you can't think that you have the knowledge and intelligence to know and accomplish it without the given companion leading you in all truth.

Your choices will determine your outcome.

Can I give you a thought? If the Holy Spirit is the Spirit of Truth and He is exclusively leading you in the ways and fulfillment of God, then all other forms of guidance will be lies. Not lies to reality but lies to your completion of purpose. Only God knows your journey. Therefore, every decision, plan, and intention should be consulted and led by the Spirit of Truth to guarantee you are reaching your purpose. Your choices will determine your outcome, so every choice you make should be carefully and intentionally considered before being made.

The Holy Spirit's guidance is an essential factor in your journey. Prayer, reading the word of God, and admittance will not facilitate keeping you moment by moment in the will of God. Understand me. I'm not telling you that those are not vital components, but the guide God gave us is our present Help in living an effective and successful walk. After prayer, the Holy Spirit reveals God's heart, and God speaks to us through the Holy Spirit. When reading the Word, it's the Holy Spirit that reveals and illuminates the revelation locked away. When you submit to the Holy Spirit, you position yourself to let the Holy Spirit work in and through you.

The Holy Spirit is essential in our knowledge of God's heart and understanding His ways and expectations. In the book of John, Jesus tells us that the Holy Spirit will teach us all things and remind us of everything He taught the disciples. This is all ultimately geared toward bringing us to Christlikeness and understanding God's plans for our lives.

With Christ's residence in our lives and the guidance and counsel of the Holy Spirit, we are but works in progress. We are continually undergoing refinement to become complete entities just as Man was created.

The Holy Spirit is our direct and constant link to God and reveals all that God wants for us in His seasons for our lives. He is the Holy Spirit, sent to convict the world of sin, guide us in all truth, and lead us in every moment of our lives. Once we receive salvation by accepting Jesus Christ in our lives as Lord, we receive the Holy Spirit who is forever with us as our guide.

In coming to this understanding, we know that we have no reason to sit back and let the devil, his schemes, or his traps dominate or control our lives. We have our guide, counselor, and protector that is more than just a voice.

OBEDIENCE

There is only one way we can truly experience the fullness of God or genuinely get to know Him better, and that is simply by being submissive and obedient. Obedience to God and His Word is essential to living a victorious and powerful Christian life in this complicated and corrupt world system.

Always remember obedience comes through humility, and humility is a choice.

To experience and know God in such an intimate manner within a relationship is only possible through total surrender and obedience to His reign. As David regularly realized during his life's journey, God is sweet and inexhaustible. Once you've tasted Him, the experience is life-changing and highly fulfilling. Obedience not only ushers in His governance in our lives, but our humility allows Him to mold us in the likeness of Christ.

Just as God instructed Moses to tell Pharaoh, "*I am the great I Am...*" whatever we need Him to be, He was, is and will be. Yes, I said was because even before you knew what you needed or even wanted He was still behind the scenes operating and being till you realized what's best and right. His revelations are given to direct us in His heart towards us and ways for us, but if not obeyed, they are simply profound words!

Christianity is built on obedience! Firstly, obedience to the call of Jesus in receiving the wonderful gift of salvation by becoming a Child of God. Secondly, obedience to the revelation of the Holy Spirit and the principles of the Word of God, to be transformed and live a fruitful and prosperous Christian life. Thirdly, obedience to follow the predestined calling of God in our life to fulfill His will on the earth.

When it comes to obedience, our greatest challenge arises when what God asks us goes against our human nature of rebelliousness and control of our destiny. The challenge comes with wanting to live on our impulses and pleasures and allowing ourselves to believe that we know best.

Life or death, success or failure, blessings or curses are all determined by our obedience or disobedience to God's word.

The second greatest challenge we suffer with obedience is being humble in all areas of our life before God. In other words, we have to give up or let go of some habits, behaviors, mindsets and people that feed our egos or gratify our desires. Obedience goes hand in hand with humility. You are either humble enough to take guidance and correction or not. There's no in-between. Often, the Holy Spirit may urge us to either terminate an activity we engage in or disconnect some friends or relationships. His goal is to bring us to a place where we are reliant upon Him and to help us avoid some of the negative situations we are prone to entertain.

Sadly, our controlling human nature rises, challenges the Holy Spirit's counsel, and wages war against the standards of God. Then, we begin to allow thoughts of self-sufficiency to arise. We must remember that the enemy will challenge us and put forward all efforts to dissuade us from following God's word. Let's consider the account of Eve in the garden and her conversation with the devil. His focus was simply on getting her to reject God's word and make a decision which she felt was good for her. Like Eve, we forget that the moment we reject God's Word, we move away from the protection of it. We also cut off the blessings connected to the obedience of it. Life or death, success or failure, blessings or curses are all determined by our obedience or disobedience to God's word. Choose wisely!

God demands radical obedience from us, especially in today's world where many unbelievers scrutinize Christians to see if their lifestyles and speech are identical. A Christian's life is the most remarkable testimony to an unbeliever. It is much more impactful than anything we can say. What we do means more than what we say. Why should unbelievers take us seriously if we claim we have all these beautiful advantages but don't want to obey Him? Would you take someone's advice if they don't take their own? To live such a powerful testimony of the goodness of God, we need to be radically obedient to the guidance of God through the Holy Spirit.

Jesus was humble before God when He was on earth. Jesus knew that despite being the son of the Creator of the Universe, He needed to walk in obedience and humility to accomplish His whole purpose.

3

THE TRIO OF TRAPS

"But every person is tempted when he is drawn away, enticed and baited by his own desires/lust/passions. Then the evil desire, when is conceived, gives birth to sin, and sin, when it is fully matured, brings forth death." (James 1:14-15)

James describes temptations as 'traps' and breaks them down into three stages:

1. Initially, we are drawn away or enticed through our evil desires.
2. These acted upon desires are then called sin.
3. And then the consequence of sin is death.

Let us take a closer look at this deadly trio of traps that have ensnared even the most mature Christian when caught unawares.

DESIRE

Desire is the beginning stage, where we are lured from our safe haven by the enemy exploiting our desires. At this stage, the enemy orchestrates and strategically targets our desires with some enticing opportunities that cause us to question our value system and ultimately divert from the path we're on. The enemy is so crafty that he places the perfect distraction in our lives, at just the ideal time to get the ideal response; actions that lead to sin.

Let me explain; when Eve was conversing with the serpent (the devil) in the garden, he was enticing her based on her natural desire to be like God. This desire was not evil, but when the action violated God's command, it became sin. If God had sanctioned the fruit she had picked, then her actions would not be sin.

Considering that, here's a thought. The devil never entices you only to gratify a desire. Every temptation is deceptively wrapped to offer you a supposedly better outcome, but the price tag is always disobedience to God. Satan will never tempt you to do anything that does not violate God's word or desires for you. Take sex, for example. If you are married, he would never tempt you to have sex with your husband or wife when you desire sex. Instead, he would tempt you to have sex outside of your spouse. This act would pervert the sexual experience with that person because it defies God's will and plans for your life.

Ultimately, the temptation is not just to give you a good time but to lure you into an act that defies God's laws for your life, leading to your destruction. The rule for Eve and Adam was the moment you eat the fruit; you will die. The consequence of their actions was death.

The devil's entire plan in tempting you to question God then act and sin is to destroy you, your relationship with God, and ultimately derail you of your journey on fulfilling your life's purpose. Always remember this, Jesus tells us in John 10:10(a), "The thief (devil) comes to steal, kill and destroy us…."

Usually, we are enticed at two moments in our lives:

1. When we are low in confidence and going through a difficult time, and become desperate for a solution.
2. When everything is going perfectly, and our confidence is high, and we become complacent.

You see, the enemy knows what makes our heart melt or what triggers us to question the right and best path for ourselves. He targets that vulnerable moment when we are least alert and protected and gives us a proposition of possibility. He makes us think and consider just like Eve when he asked her if God really told her not to eat of the tree. Essentially the devil causes us to assess if following God's command is really in our best interest? Wouldn't it be better to disobey the command and make your own decision?

Once that connection to the heart is made, the enticement begins to intensify. Everything surrounding that desire becomes the focal point of our lives. We become distracted from our walk by the illusion of happiness or satisfaction and quickly find ourselves in a situation that seems beneficial and appropriate for us. In that momentary satisfaction, we fail to notice that the enemy has effectively lured us deep into the heart of the trap by our desires. We want to satisfy the flesh.

"Our desires become the priority of our lives rather than God's desires for us."

SIN

By this time, the enemy has successfully created the perfect satisfaction or illusion of a person, thing, or situation that can sufficiently hold our focus. Usually, our mentality is one of passivity and total naivete to the severity of our trap. We are now operating in our carnal mode, satisfying the desires that please us. Our defenses and alertness are down, replaced by thoughts of a pleasing outcome to desires in full throttle.

The devil draws us deeper into his custom-made trap, and the choice before us is no longer between right and wrong, but how best can I fulfill this desire? We fail to realize that the actual decision is either to indulge in the sinful act of pleasing self or walk in righteousness and please God.

Amazingly, even in these most vulnerable situations, God still displays His unconditional love for us. He even offers an escape that will allow us to be faithful to Him.

Have you ever been about to sin, and something occurred that distracted or stopped you from sinning, and you thought or said, "great timing?" A phone call came through, a person showed up uninvited, or a bizarre incident occurred that needed your urgent attention? Well, think of that as the escape route God provided because He realized that you could not resist the temptation on your own.

Once at the crossroads of decision, our minds race with thoughts as we consider the pros and cons of the sinful act we feel so enticed to make. Our palms become sweaty, our hearts become heavy, and the flesh is greedy with desires for pure gratification. Fleetingly, you weigh the options: either indulge the moment and enjoy the gratification or just walk away. All this internal reasoning fails, and because of our desires and desperation or complacency at this point, we indulge.

We have now experienced the full progression of intensified passion and desires that our fleshly lust has fueled. In the Desire stage, there is no sin committed – we are only tormented by deliberation and possibilities. However, the fleshly desires consume us at this sin stage, and indulgence is now a reality.

At this moment as well, we hear the Holy Spirit speaking urgently to us about our sinful practices. The Holy Spirit reiterates God's disapproval and shows us how we can be free from the grasp of the enemy. Sadly, by this time, our flesh is thriving, so we struggle to silence the voice of the Holy Spirit because of the guilt and disappointment we now face.

This puts us in an uncomfortable paradox. Although we may be physically enjoying the indulgence, this stage is always quite tumultuous. Not only do we feel very irritated and miserable on the inside, but our life begins to become problematic and challenging. We find ourselves off track from God's path and trapped because we now see our error but are trapped in a decision that has consequences.

Looking back at James 1:15, we accept that everything we do starts with a desire that births a thought. Only when the idea is acted upon does it become a reality and become an obsession. The same applies to sin: it begins as a desire and manifests in our minds as a thought that is simply a response to our desires. Once that thought is acted upon, it becomes a sin, and that sin is practiced and enjoyed, thus giving way to it becoming a habit.

Sinful acts produce disconnection from God and ultimately cause death. Death is not just physical but refers to anything that's disconnected from an intimate relationship with God. Dead speaks to not having spiritual intimacy with God and being without purpose. In other words, being barren or devoid of purpose!

I also think I need to take a moment to tell you that spiritual intimacy is not regulated by man's terms but by God's terms. We cannot decide what is acceptable to us and tell God what the order will be. Just like in the garden, after the perfect creation, God established an order to have intimacy with Him; obey His word. We cannot decide to negate His word or even choose what's acceptable or workable for us and then expect God to be okay with it. His standard is Holiness, which is not measured or determined by us because it accommodates our lifestyles or beliefs. Get to know what His Word states, and as a result, you will discover what God's expectation is for us to have an intimate relationship with Him.

DEATH

The final stage is the stage of extremity! We are now entirely ensnared by the enemy's trap. We indulge in sin, enjoy the illusion of total gratification in its fullness, and are derailed from walking in God's word. Of course, the more we indulge, the further we drift from the intimate relationship with God. Our spiritual desires are dulled, and if we constantly indulge, eventually, they will become dormant.

The feeling of guilt now reaches its fullest, and it is quite interesting how it operates. The feelings of guilt manifest, but not just a sense of guiltiness towards our sinful acts, but we also feel too ashamed to return to God and ask for forgiveness. We are embarrassed and go into a self-preservation mode where we try to fix it our way.

Once again, the devil has gained the upper hand in feeding our thoughts despite our awareness of God's increasing reminder of His expectation. Like in the Garden, He makes Himself known to us by calling out to us. What I've realized, though, is that God was not calling out to Adam and Eve for them to give Him their location but rather to reveal His.

"They heard the sound of the LORD God walking in the garden in the cool of the day, and the man and his wife hid themselves from the presence of the LORD God among the trees of the garden. Then the LORD God called to the man, and said to him, "Where are you?"- Genesis 3:8-9

I mentioned that when we are being tempted that God provides an option out of the trap. Revealing His location let Adam and Eve know that He was near, and asking for them meant He was still caring for them. He already knew what they did because He's omniscient. Hence, the question was not one to ascertain location but one of explanation. He knows when we sin and knows we are in a state of guilt and hiding, but He still comes after us because He loves us even when we reject Him.

Here's the principle. God didn't just turn up on them and say here's what we will do. He always gives us the chance to repent and come back to Him. This means that He never takes away our will by forcing us, but our decision to take the step back says that we are committing to our restoration. God always responds to our need for help, but He never imposes. He just stays close, letting us know that nothing can separate us from His love. As David tells us in Psalms 139 verse 8, even if he makes the worse decision and ends up in hell-like situations, God is still close.

Even at your lowest, most sinful stage, God will always be trying to get your attention–still allowing you to redeem yourself by answering, repenting, and returning to Him. As we drift farther and farther and refuse God's call for our redemption, we allow death to permeate our lives and affect everything.

The Death stage is, unfortunately, where many Christians exist today. They just exist by attending church Sunday after Sunday, hearing an excellent emotional sermon, and merely going through the motions of Christianity but not addressing the law of sin and death. Death cannot be willed away. It must be disarmed and replaced by another authority and lived out: Life.

I know this sounds really contrary to be in death stage as a Believer but death does not speak to physical death. When God told Adam and Eve the moment they eat from the tree they will die they did. Not physically but spiritually. So here the death now is not spiritually because salvation restores our relationship with God and revives our spirits that were dead. But one major death that also occurred in the garden was death to purpose. Many of us are alive but still not alive to our purpose and this is where the ultimate life is manifested. Christ refers to it as Abundant Life. Like the Rich Young Ruler in Matthew 19:16-22, who came to Christ inquiring about Eternal Life. Jesu told Him to enter Life obey and honor His commandments and he said to Jesus he was bur what is he still lacking.

This statement totally shifts the narrative now because it now implies there has to be more than obeying the laws of God as a Believer. So then Jesus tells him if you want to be perfect [enter Abundant Life] you have to go sell all you have and come and follow him. This grieved the Young Ruler because it was not just about the money but was really about letting go of all that he knew, was and identified with and come start over a whole new life that's focused on Purpose and God's will for your life. This may sound similar to salvation but I assure you is far more. This is the Abundant Life gift that Christ declared he came to give in John 10:10.

There one thing to come into salvation but please understand it's another thing to pursue purpose through Christ.

Yes I'm saying to you that as Believers many us have become comfortable in the excitement of having Eternal Life because we have been too long been cultured that that is the ultimate gift but I want to tell you it's a great gift but there is an even bigger and better gift inside that gift. It's called fulfilling purpose. Look at man's genesis. Form the garden it was decided to make man to fulfil a purpose set by God nut just to claim intimacy with God. Man always had an assignment set by God and it's to be Fruitful and Multiply and have dominion over the earth. Let me put it in this way. Having a relationship with God positions you as a child of God but walking out His principles ordained for us affords us the authority to fulfil purpose.

Galatians 4:1 tells us that a child even though he's an heir has as much authority as a slave so there is a tutor placed over him to educate and culture him in three areas that prepares hm for the authority granted to the Son.

1: *Who the Father is as King*
2: *Who he is as a Son and the expectations of the Father towards him*
3: *The culture of the Kingdom that he must know and operate in to be who he is called to be*

Being Alive is great but what's better than great? Well let's say Life in Abundance! Don't just be comfortable being in Christ, strive to fulfil through Him. I know that many of us are in a stage that the Rich Young Ruler existed. You have been obeying but still has a desire that there is more but can't grasp what and where to find it. I implore you, like the young man did run to God and ask Him what must you do to get in that place. What must you get rid of. What or who must you unhinge yourself from to follow after your purpose. Where must you be repositioned to be able to be nurtured to become that person God intends. It is where your fulfilment lies.

Can I give you another though? Christ must be seen as more than Salvation. The embodiment of Purpose. And if we are in Him we too must be purpose manifested. He is far more than a Savior who is there to help you through life. He's come to give you more than Life. He's come to give you Abundant Life. Purpose.

"Knowing God will position you but living in Him will prosper you in all fulness of life."

By the time we reach this point, the devil's trap would have worked successfully, and we are no longer a threat to his plans of destruction. We are no longer passionate for God as we settle for living in sin and accept the difficulties and oppression, which the enemy brings to all areas of our lives. We settle for operating in the flesh and seek to satisfy its every desire, and we no longer live in the victory the Christ died to give us. Mere survival and existence are our versions of living life. But is it? Did God create us just to exist or to live out a purpose that shows forth His glory?

Having previously experienced the glory of living in Christ, you must examine yourself in the death stage. You must ask, "Is this any way to live as a Christian who tasted the awesomeness of God's presence in my life? If we could only bring ourselves to repent in this stage, we would touch God's heart immeasurably as He asks where we are and return to Him.

Here's another thing about the stage of death: It may not come instantly, but it will come. I guarantee it. God's word does not just fade away but will always fulfill what He spoke. Adam and Eve experienced instant spiritual death in separation from God, but the real impact of sin occurred over the next 900 plus years of their existence. They paid the penalty for sin by being expelled from the garden, which meant their perfect home was lost, but even worse, it wasn't recovered.

They lost their dominion over the earth and now had to labor to survive. They lost their identity. They lost the ability to love deeply because God is love, and only true love spawns from God. As a result, their relationships were cursed with conflict. They lost their sense of value and settled for a state that was far below God's plan.

The two most significant consequences they faced that affect us up to this day were the loss of capacity and ability to fulfill their purpose. Purpose fulfillment is only known through and by God. As we would later see in the following few Genesis chapters, Adam and Eve also cursed their children, and Cain killed Abel out of jealousy and anger. Yes, our sins can affect our children and even their children.

4

STRENGTH IN UNITY

Everyone needs a friend. There is no better time to be a true friend and lend support, prayer, or whatever is necessary than when someone is in the midst of his or her trials. Friends are not there to take you out of your trials but just to be a support system and sometimes a messenger from God.

Despite how strong a person may seem or how focused on God they are, there is nothing like the support or well-timed encouragement of a companion or close friend. I believe that Paul had such a friend to call on and talk to in his moments of distress. And Paul certainly had his moments of distress and trials! In Romans 12:5, he encourages us to *"Rejoice with those who rejoice and mourn with those who mourn."* No one can relate to another in the depths of mourning or join them in their moments of rejoicing unless they are intimate in the person's life and situation.

When Jesus was in the Garden of Gethsemane, and He was in prayer to the point of blood dripping from his pores, why do you think He went back to the disciples and asked them "why they couldn't stay awake and pray?" It was not because He was unable to handle His task alone, but physically, His flesh yearned for the support of His closest friends. It is okay for us to rely on friends during trials. Of course, they don't usually take the difficulties away, but their consistent presence and encouragement can make a huge difference.

I was going through a personal trial, and I can tell you that a companion's support is priceless. There was a commercial for Visa credit card years ago that presented all kinds of situations and items that money can buy and the commercial ended by telling us some things are priceless. Love is priceless, a smile is priceless, and support from a friend or companion is priceless.

In my low times and struggles, I continued to pray and applied God's principles. I kept an attitude of joyousness and employed all the strategies and methods I mentioned earlier. Still, there was nothing like the hug and small words of encouragement I received from my wife at the time. Even when she could not offer answers or solutions, I needed her unconditional support. Her presence in my life at that point meant a great deal to me, and her confidence that I would make it through the trials strengthened me even more.

Now that does not negate the need for the Holy Spirit that Christ said will be our Comforter, but Christ was full of the Holy Spirit and still had friends. Friends are essential, and the only thing you need to do is make wise choices in friends and know that all friends are not for all situations.

Thankfully, the same God who we accept is all-sufficient is also all-understanding and encourages us to value earthly support. Whether it is from a spouse, companion, relative, or just a close friend, we need to understand that we were created to be in a community. God commanded Adam and Eve to go and multiply and inhabit the earth. We need friends to make it in and through this life.

5

SAME GAME, SAME TACTICS, SAME SIN

Although 1 Corinthians 10:13 states, "*...no temptation has seized you that is not common to man...*" it is also important to understand that the temptation is uniquely designed to entice each individual according to their personal " Lust of the Flesh."

The devil's tricks and schemes of today are not any different than in Bible times. He is very precise and focuses his attacks on the situations and practices that we struggle with. Whether they are spiritual, sexual, financial, relational, or emotional, the enemy will specially craft a trap catered to our desires.

Thankfully, I Corinthian 10:13 continues, "*...and God is faithful; He will not let you be tempted beyond what you can bear. But when you are tempted, he will also provide a way out so that you can stand up under it.*"

It is comforting and overwhelming to know that God will still come after us offering an escape route back home to Him despite our selfishness and disobedience. He loves us unconditionally.

In the famous book of Job, before the devil could do anything to Job, he needed to seek God's permission. The same applies to our lives today: nothing happens to us unless God allows it. Even though the devil may have a full-fledged attack planned, he can only do as much as God allows.

I must also state something here because God has given us the privilege to choose. We have the power to choose right (Obedience to God) or wrong (Disobedience). Each choice comes with the blessing or curse of the law we either honor or defy. This was the part of the truth the enemy purposely neglected to tell Eve. Just as Adam and Eve experienced the penalty of disobedience, they would have also experienced the results of obedience. Life is built on the choices we make.

We should always keep in mind that the Lord constantly uses the devil's schemes and traps to bring honor and glory to His name by displaying His mighty and handy work through and for us. In every trap and scheme orchestrated by the enemy, the Lord extends grace, and we always end up with the situation in our favor.

And we know that in all things God works for the good of those who love him, who have been called according to his purpose. - (Romans 8 vs. 28)

I must tell you, though, that you must stay close to God and completely follow His direction to see this kind of favor manifest in its fullness. I know right now you may be asking yourself why the Lord even allows the devil to attack or try to trap us, but God's plans for us have always superseded the devil's schemes. Through God, Satan's schemes will work to our benefit.

Chapter 1 of the book of Job begins by stating, *"Job was righteous and upright in all his ways..."* which can be reworded to say that Job trusted in God and walked righteously before Him. Later in verse 8, God refers to Job as His servant, which implies that Job served Him faithfully and God trusted Job's loyalty to Him. That is the level of relationship that God desires with us where He can be confident in our loyalty to Him despite the situation.

Job 1:12 goes on to imply that God allowed Job to be attacked by the devil. We have already discussed James 1:14, which says that our evil desires tempt us. Are these two verses contradictory? No. God allows the devil to tempt us after we have proven that we can be trusted by being refined and overcoming God's designed trials for our lives. It is at this point that God says with complete confidence in us to the devil: *"...have you considered my servant; he is faithful and righteous in all his ways?"*

The Lord says this with complete confidence in our loyalty. He allows the devil to attempt to trap us in a particular area in which we have matured and been refined in. It is in these attacks, which lead to schemed temptations that we, like Job, can authoritatively say, "*Our God is faithful, and we will not betray Him by succumbing to our fleshly desire and evil lust.*" Like Job, we should be prepared to stand firmly in our righteousness despite what comes our way.

These traps could come smack in the middle of our trials to trap and derail us and come at the end of our success in overcoming a trial. They are then allowed to illuminate what we need to address in ourselves. If you see the complete account of Job in chapter 40, Job declared his ears once heard, but now his eyes have seen God. In other words, Job now had a better vision and relationship with God as a result of his experience.

Traps are also allowed to prove to us (and the enemy) that we have triumphed over a particular weakness and are no longer bound by it. Think of it this way: God uses the devil's traps as an exam to test your studying and preparation, knowing that you will pass with flying colors!

6

THE SETUP

The enemy realizes your spiritual comfort and quickly creates a situation where something catches your attention (whatever you have a liking for in the time or phase of life.) Let's suppose that it is a job or position offering the money you want so much. Imagine that it has all the perks and benefits that would supposedly make you feel comfortable.

Having begun the job, you become aware of someone who unexpectedly begins to help and advise you, gives you constant attention, and eventually their phone number. This person appeals to you as the most attractive and sweet individual you could ever hope to know. You begin to develop a "harmless" friendship that flourishes as the two of you work together. Daily you communicate via messaging, have lunch together, and often share transportation or travel on the same bus route. You eventually begin going out at night after work and weekends together.

Let me pause here and say that if God blesses us and we ill-treat it or do not steward it correctly, destruction is coming. The devil will make maximum use of our momentary distraction from God and make it become the focus of our life and ultimately a full-time distraction. When that happens, we have allowed the blessing to become demonized and have opened an avenue for the devil to corrupt or destroy the good gift God has blessed us with. Satan jumps at every opportunity when we allow a blessing to be a distraction which opens a doorway for traps to lead to our demise. Now let's return to the scenario.

Your attraction for this person is being satisfied. Simultaneously, your intimacy with God is suffering because this person is now your number one focus. Imagine that you eventually find yourself in a compromising situation where you are alone with that (harmless) most appealing person. This person then urges you to indulge in an act that will lead to your demise.

The devil is not dumb. He knew that you had desires and even struggles and cleverly orchestrated that chain of events to lure us away from our safety zone into a place of vulnerability and compromise.

Have you ever seen any of the movies from the franchise entitled "Final Destination?" The movies are based on the theory that we cannot cheat death, and when it is your time to die, it will happen inevitably. What stood out to me in the movies was how the producer orchestrated accidents, or for lack of a better word, traps, that set the stage to ensure the individual's death.

Similarly, the devil orchestrated the initial meeting, knowing that the person's values were opposite to yours. He knew that your desires and weaknesses would be tested, leading to a series of events that would culminate in traps. You have now come to a situation where there is no one around, and you have no spiritual shelter from the barrage of the enemy. Yes, you were lured away. Furthermore, you have no strength to stand up against the temptation because you are spiritually weak, weary, and desensitized.

Your flesh is now dominating, and the desires are raging. All you feel is the yearning to fulfill that fleshly craving. Your cravings begin to control your decisions, and you give more and more consideration to just enjoying the moment (sin). "Just this once!" You say, but what was once a trial of controlling your youthful lust by applying God's principles has evolved into a situation that catapults you into the valley of decision between sin and righteousness.

Temptations do not necessarily come directly, but as seen above, they can occur at the end of a series of events that are (supposedly) innocent!

The devil plays tag with you until you are entirely comfortable and unaware that you have been dreamily pulled along. And then you wake up and find yourself "smack dab" in the middle of a well-brewed temptation!

When I was a kid, I remember my mom always preached to me, "Never play with strangers!" I only obeyed this advice out of sheer fear of my mother's wrath, but now that I am a man and a mature Christian, I understand the dual implications of this warning.

In the physical sense, a stranger can come and portray a very kind and safe environment. When you are comfortable, they can spring all kinds of traps on you to ensnare you. This kind of scenario is not only limited to children. It is also present in the adult world where an innocent-looking person enters your life and befriends you with all kinds of hidden agendas. After they have "lured you to sleep" or "broke down your defenses" and acquired your trust, they take full advantage of your trust and trick you into all kinds of calamities.

Likewise, the devil entices you with all kinds of possessions or persons that appeal to your sense of security and trust. People come into your life, befriend you, earn your trust, and impress you with all kinds of qualities and even possibilities of what they can do for you. They seek to earn your trust and cause you to lower your defenses, and lure you right into the heart of a trap that causes much hurt, embarrassment, and disgrace. This trap then leaves your personal life in disarray and your Christian integrity tarnished.

Many persons enter your life who seem to have great motives. They appear all friendly and sincere when they have ulterior motives that always climax in sinful traps we never expected. We must come to the reality that the devil uses persons, just like possessions, to distract and divert us from our walk with God and pursuit of purpose. They may have sincere motives but sincere to who? Never take the thief for granted. Anything that can be used to stop you from coming into your fullness will be used in any way.

Christians can be so naïve at times because we want to see the good, and that's not a bad thing. We always think that everything is so genuine and pure because everything comes from God. I always tell my friends, "If you are not for the Lord, you are for the devil," and this is in the Word. We must allow time to nurture and reveal all things, and most of all, let the Holy Spirit guide us even in relationships. He's our guide and the revealer of all truths. Stop trying to navigate your life on your own, and then when you need help, try to solicit the Holy Spirit's guidance. God is interested in every little thing about you. Let Him guide you, and you'll see the deception is not as easy. The problem with this is we have to give up our "it's my life" mode and realize it's God's life that we gave back to Him.

The devil can also use fellow Christians to deter or distract you from your purposed path even with the best intentions. The reality is, once it is not in alignment with God's spoken Word to you, it will derail you. Let no one contradict God's Word in your life and try to convince you to go against it. They are operating in the role of the serpent that the devil was manipulating. If anyone is trying to get you to oppose God's Word, Stop and Step back. Realize that the thief is in operation trying to set a trap to bring you down and Paul tells us in Ephesians 6:12 to look far beyond the flesh and realize *"we wrestle not against flesh or blood, but against principalities, against powers, against the rulers of darkness of this age, against spiritual host of wickedness in the heavenly places."* Don't just operate at face value, be wise and spiritually discerning.

7

EVEN WHEN WE STUMBLE

One comforting thing to remember is that our Father only allows us to face what He knows we can handle once we walk in tune with His guidance. By allowing each trial to come to us, God proves what we can do once we move outside of our limited realm of thinking and make a step of faith. It was this way in Peter's case when he stepped off the boat onto the water. Peter had to go far beyond what his rational mind could conceive and rely on what God commanded him to do. He had to have faith in Jesus' ability to do whatever he was commanded to do.

Let me state that there are always persons, thoughts and even experiences that will tell us, "The reality is...." Know, however, that the reality is what God says it is. Those persons or thoughts limit you to the natural and what they can see and think, but God operates in the supernatural. We must not reduce God's Word to us to rationalization or corporate opinion but take Him for what He says. He never lies, He never fails, and God never aborts us! When you are faced with "the reality is…" obstacles or persons, ask yourself what's God's reality for me. Is it what you see or think or what God says it is or will be?

Our true potential is revealed when we step out of the boat in faith and let go of our sense of security. We must believe that the same God who commanded us to step out will also keep us safely above water level. *God will ALWAYS complete a good work that He has begun in us...He NEVER aborts His Word.*

Peter's faith allowed him to walk on water, and even more significantly, allowed him to do what the world would have told him was impossible.

I like to call this evolution moving from Having Faith to Becoming Faith. You see, Peter had faith to step off the boat, but you would realize that this step of faith allowed him to act like the person he had faith in. Peter adopted and adapted to the source of his faith, but Peter's faith had to evolve because it was also this faith evolved that had to keep him on the water. If you read the account, you will see that Christ asked Peter why he had so little faith and why he doubted.

This question had two levels. Why does Peter doubt the source, that source that called him, and why does he doubt his ability to do what he was told to do by the faith that is in him. Christ wanted Peter to realize he could not just have faith to step, but he needed to become faith to sustain and accomplish the walk. Christ wanted Peter to realize that it was his faith that made walking on water possible.

Like the rest of us, the challenge Peter initially encountered was the rationalization of the actions God commanded of him. We allow our minds and fears to take over and limit our faith from empowering us to do what God tells us. We then limit God's power in our lives and ultimately determine our intimacy with Him. Peter allowed his physical perceptions to frame the situation, and as a result, began to entertain the possibility of failure and began to sink, just like we do.

We all tend to start our trials with great passion and belief in God. Still, as difficulties present themselves, as the wind and waves begin to rage, we often panic and entertain doubts about God's capabilities, abilities, and promises. We ultimately start to question our ability to accomplish or fulfill the assignment.

When we display a lack of confidence in God, we then lose confidence in ourselves. When we hesitate, we deliberate, and deliberation opens us up to disobey, and when we disobey, we sin. When doubts arise during our trials, we alternatively seek rational, self-manufactured options and methods to deal with our trials. We choose these methods rather than sticking to the promise God gave to us at the beginning. We are quick to abort God because of our fears and what persons are advising us to do.

The more we abort God's process, the longer we remain babes in Him and are more vulnerable to the devil's traps and their success. Once we correlate this vulnerability to our distance from God's presence, we begin to panic, and our obedience to God is further compromised. Panic signals fear, which is a reflection of doubt, and as indicated earlier, doubt opens the door to disobedience that leads us right back to sin!

We all are limited in ourselves, but when we allow God's anointing to empower our abilities, we can begin to walk above the parameters of the world. We live in the world but should not allow the world to dictate where, when, and how we operate in our efforts to respond to God's calling on our lives. Christians must always walk in the Christ system if we are to succeed in what we do.

They are not of the world, even as I am not of it. – John 17:16

If we had as much confidence in God as He has in us, we would sidestep many of Satan's traps - particularly those activated by our panic, doubts, or fears.

When you try to decipher the order of God's directions and operations, you will always be confused because we can never comprehend Him. We can only know His nature, which is to be faithful to bring to pass all He has begun. One person's journey will never be another's, but be assured that we must all have two things in common; humility and faith.

8

HARD BOILED FROG

I attended an Apostolic Men's Summit in July of 2004. There, I was blown away by the presence of God amongst the men for the entire weekend. The passion, reverence, humility, openness, bonding, love, and most of all, the impartation of knowledge was beyond explanation and account. One of the many lessons learned by every man who attended this summit was a principle called "The Boiled Frog Mentality" that many men fall victim to. This tactic used by the enemy is not just used on men, as you will see shortly, but on all people in various situations.

What is "The Boiled Frog Mentality?" If you caught a frog and dropped it into a tub of hot water, it would quickly realize the water temperature and leap out to protect its life. Amazingly, if you placed that same frog in a tub of cold water and slowly increased the heat until it began to boil, the frog would eventually die. Why? The frog instantly recognized the already hot water would harm him and sought to escape, but when the water gradually heated up, the frog could not detect the danger, and eventually, it was too late. The frog's senses never noticed that the once comfortable and even pleasurable surroundings were now extremely dangerous and life-ending. His desensitization to his surroundings caused him to become a Hard-Boiled Frog.

This simple and profound "real" experiment with the frog really gave me a new paradigm shift when it comes to human beings, Christians especially, and the mentality that causes our demise. We can react to the very sight of danger or entrapment at a split second. It is the slow-cooked, slow schemed, slowly built-up traps and hazards that easily elude us. Before we know it, we are consumed and destroyed by what we thought was a safe and harmless circumstance.

I left that summit telling myself that I had to learn and protect against this tactic the enemy successfully uses against us in our lives and share it with others. I must admit that I had a full, practical experience of being a Hard-Boiled Frog despite having learned the theory of the tactic. My painful experience forced me to acquire applicable principles that can help you escape the trap of being Hard Boiled in your surroundings. Please take serious note of these principles because a wise man learns from a fool's mistakes. From my experience of being boiled, I learned three major principles:

1: *Take the advice of one who is outside looking in.*
2: *Be totally open and honest*
3: *Be deliberate with your actions of escape*

TAKING ADVICE

We often fall due to pride and arrogance even when we are not aware that we act in these ways. My fiancée at the time came to me when I was leisurely moving along in my circumstance and spelled out the dangers that I was standing in. But, because I could not see the threat due to pride and internal blindness, I believed that I was in tune enough with the Holy Spirit to see any dangers if they aroused. Total Mistake! Before I could catch a hint of trouble, the hot water was already at boiling point. I have always heard persons say it is always different when outside looking in, versus inside looking out, and you know what? It is so true!

When there is someone who loves and has your best interest at heart standing on the outside telling you that there is trouble brewing like a hurricane, trust them. They can see it more clearly, especially when they are Christians walking plugged into God and their emotions are not influencing decisions.

Many times our decision-making is disabled because we are emotionally high jacked and irrational. We are emotionally fueled, and our decision is made based on the emotions that are ruling at the moment. Be very careful of this state because it can lead to being emotionally kidnapped. This is where you find yourself being so emotionally damaged through experiences that you devoid yourself of healthy emotional experiences and operate in a very disconnected place. This is the other extreme.

Your vision becomes blinded by your desires or the pride of thinking you can handle it. There is nothing wrong with heeding advice even though you are not able to see or understand. If you know God has placed persons in your life to help and support you, be humble and take their advice. I confess that after learning this principle in totality, I told my fiancée that even if I could not see what she was telling me, I would humble myself and listen to her advice. I promised to take it and act upon it because I know she had my best interest at heart and loved me. I would not even debate or rationalize it. She loved me, and my welfare was a priority to her, and that is all I needed to know.

Men, we value our women and their placement in our lives, but we don't fully allow them to be who they really are. One excellent quality a woman has is her ability to discern and recognize the enemy, so stop being proud and humble yourself with your partner. Besides, pride goes before the fall, and many times it's not that the trap was that cleverly schemed, but rather it was our pride that blinded us from seeing clearly and caused our fall.

TOTAL OPENNESS AND HONESTY

Openness breeds honesty. Honesty breeds a healthy relationship, and a healthy relationship produces strength and protection from the devil's schemes. I will emphasize transparency and honesty because anything that needs to be done in the dark or be hidden is not entirely wholesome. The act is either contradictory to the relationship or contradictory to your integrity. If we seek to be people whose words and actions are congruent, we have to be open books. Being a person of righteousness and integrity is simply being an individual of selflessness and total submission to the Word. We must be honest! That cannot even be discussed or rationalized. Our word is more valuable to us than money, and it must be what we stand on. The moment we are not operating in integrity, we are seen as untrustworthy, and the value of loyalty is not given to us.

BEING DELIBERATE WITH YOUR
ACTIONS OF ESCAPE

You cannot tip-toe around the facts. You are either moving forward or staying, and you are either sinning or walking righteously. There is no neutral place! Often, we try to appease our laziness or disobedience with the theory of process. In reality, we are not doing anything to get to the next level but still indulging in the traps and bondages destroying us.

We have all been in positions where we tried to convince ourselves that we will eventually stop. How does that truly end? We soon find out the only remedy is the brutal cold- turkey approach. We have to stop and deal with the triggers that keep us desiring to indulge.

We must become persons of intentionality and deliberately do what needs to be done to get where we need to get. The more we tolerate, the more we compromise, and the stronghold of sin keeps us trapped and broken. You cannot entertain flirtation with the enemy and still think you will come out unscathed.

If Eve had cut the conversation short with the devil and not entertained the ideas he was giving her, we would have a different outcome. Sometimes entertaining the devil is why we end up in the trap, and the truth is, we entertain him because it appeals to a desire we have.

9

THE RESCUE

When Peter began to sink, he panicked, and you can imagine all the thoughts that were bombarding his mind. Thoughts of drowning, even as much as questioning Jesus' motive for calling him out of the boat. Peter probably wondered if Christ had set him up to drown(fail).

I'm sure that Peter's thoughts mirrored those which we have had at some point in time. You see, when we encounter difficulties and problems within our trials, we tend to blame everyone and everything and question God's reasons for allowing us to go through such harrowing ordeals. It is easy to overlook the fact that we cause ourselves to suffer because of disobedience. We feel lost, alone, and a sense of abandonment, and still, like Peter, we continue to sink further. It is precisely at this time that we need to look to Christ for our rescue and focus on Him just as Peter did, or we will surely keep sinking. (James 1:14-15).

We must remember God's first Word in all situations to us and obey it in its fullness. God's commands within the trials may seem impractical to us and, many times, impossible to see the rationale. If we only respond with radical obedience rather than doubts and intelligence, we will never go wrong.

Letting our trials consume us only makes us more vulnerable to the progression of deceptions and traps laid by the devil, placed to diminish our strength. Amid these trials, the more we lose focus on God, the more we begin to operate in the flesh. Of course, this chain of events guarantees our defeat and sure victory for the devil.

Our perspective determines our response and our results. Thus, if we view the trials as an evil, bad experience, they will be responded to as such. James tells us to count it a joy when you face trials, not because you are a sadist but because you understand God is not trying to harm you but mature and equip you. Your perspective precedes your response, and your response determines your behaviors and posture to learn and grow.

Throughout the Psalms, David mentions our need to wait on God continually. He tells us we should wait on God for guidance and spiritually prepare for the next move. He suggests we do this through dedication in studying His Word, listening to the counsel of the Holy Spirit, and then acting on His commands without hesitation as He gives them. This kind of radical obedience helps keep our eyes, mind, and heart focused on God's path for us.

Then Isaiah tells us in chapter 40:31, *"But those who hope in the LORD will renew their strength. They will soar on wings like eagles; they will run and not grow weary, they will walk and not be faint."* Essentially, this tells us that waiting on God will guarantee us a renewed strength that will allow us to operate on another level and not get weary or give up.

Waiting on the Lord is not procrastinating or being lazy. It's like when Christ told the disciples to wait in Jerusalem until they received the power to do what He called and prepared them to do. Waiting is allowing God to give you the authority to operate in His will at His time. This has a lot more to unpack, but I will summarize it with this. While they waited, they were in eager preparation, praying, consecrating themselves, and submitting themselves to the command of Christ in anticipation of the endowment. They were waiting and ready.

10

ALL THAT GLITTERS
IS NOT GOLD

I often remember the stray cat that chose to become a family member without invitation when I was a kid despite my family's disapproval. Whenever we left food for our dogs, we would see the cat stride proudly up to the bowl and begin to eat. It did not matter if we were there watching or whether the dogs were already eating; the cat would boldly approach the food bowl and demand his share. Even if the dogs fought him off, the cat would snarl and fight back until we intervened and chased him away. This went on for some time, but the cat always returned the next day despite our best efforts.

Eventually, my Dad decided to catch him and take him to the animal shelter. This, however, was much easier said than done! Whenever Daddy tried to catch him, the cat would outrun and outsmart my dad in every way. We always got a laugh from watching this cat draw Daddy into running him all through the house and yard to no avail. After a while, it appeared that the cat was toying with Daddy. Out of incredible frustration, Daddy devised a new strategy. Daddy decided to befriend the cat and got it to trust him, knowing that he would be able to take him up and carry him to the shelter gently.

Daddy started to leave out milk and food in separate containers for the cat, executing his new plan. If he was eating a meal and saw the cat, he would also toss him some of whatever he was eating for the cat to give him the impression of love. For about a week, this went on until one day when Daddy was at the dinner table, the cat walked up to daddy's leg, rubbed against it, and purred for food. I saw Daddy smile and say, "Gotcha!" Daddy wasted no time and reached down, picked up the cat, and took him straight to the shelter.

The process of befriending the cat took some time. Still, it was much more effective because the cat eventually felt safe enough to walk up to Daddy without reservation, with all defenses down. This was precisely what Daddy wanted because otherwise, the cat would have continued to use its defenses --- speed, claws, and leaping abilities, to keep away from Daddy.

That simple entrapment scenario provides us with a better idea of how the enemy sets out to lure us into a state of relaxation and trust. When our defenses are finally down, he pounces all over us and traps us. When we are alert, we can discern, pray, rebuke, and cast down the strongholds the enemy tries to set up against us. Would you do all that to a 'friend' whom you trusted and cared for? I am sure you wouldn't, and the enemy knows this just the same!

Therefore, we must fight the enemy's visible attacks and recognize the devious and friendly forms the enemy uses to get behind our walls of defense.

Paul tells us we are not battling with flesh or blood but rather in the spiritual. With this understanding, we need to capture a few truths, which I will list below:

1. The physical is not important and can be a distraction to what you are truly up against.
2. To be spiritually successful, you must be spiritually discerning and aware.
3. If the spiritual is the place we need to focus on, we need to be spiritually prepared and capable.
4. Paul tells us in 2 Corinthians 10:4 that we cannot fight spiritual warfare with physical weapons.
5. The spiritual realm operates and respects authority and not association. When the sons of Sceva in Acts 19:11-20 went to expel evil spirits, the spirits asked them who they were. The spirits stated Jesus they knew, Paul they knew but not them, and as a result, the sons of Sceva were mercilessly beaten.
6. Only when we are aware, equipped, and alert will we defeat the enemy in his schemes and trap setting.

11

ACCEPTING THE CHALLENGE

One thing we Christians had better come to grips with is we are and will always be tried and tested until we are like Christ. Until then, we should always be ready to face the trials that help us move closer and closer towards Christ-likeness in being a Son.

A long time ago, in a movie called "Marked for Death" starring Steven Seagal, I heard the phrase, "Everybody wants to go to heaven, but nobody wants to die." That phrase reflects the type of mentality many Christians live with; they all want to be Christ-like, but they do not want to be refined to His likeness through the testing and refinement of trials(die). Unfortunately, most human beings want to acquire everything with the least possible amount of struggle or discomfort. The rude awakening comes when you realize that this mentality is unacceptable in life, especially in Christianity.

Unless the renewal of the mind takes place and an acceptance of trials is made, Christians can never come into their fullness in God. You see, it is a catch-22. With every trial that you endure, you are brought closer to Christ's likeness, and you come into your predestined purpose. As you overcome each trial, your mind is progressively renewed, and you begin to see life and its actual realities through the eyes of Christ.

The most challenging task of this refinement process is going through the uncertainty and despair while keeping your eyes fixed on God and His promises. You may think that you cannot last or that you have not been a Christian long enough to show such faith, but indeed you can! Just refer to Romans 12:12, where Paul gives a tremendous Three-Step Attitude to getting through trials: *"Have an attitude of hope; be patient in trials and be faithful in prayer."* Like most of Paul's advice, this verse is worthy of closer examination.

12

THREE STEPS TO ENDURING

HAVE AN ATTITUDE OF HOPE

To have an overcoming attitude of hope is to have a positive and sure attitude about the outcome of every situation. This is only possible once we understand our Father's faithfulness, capabilities, unconditional love, and ultimate plan for us. We also must be open to accepting the love which He is offering. Receiving God's love should also mean being open to His ways and predestined will for our lives. When we receive God, we profess that we are giving Him reign over our lives to reform us to Christ-likeness. Reliance on God should be total and without boundaries or fears.

This will introduce the principle of Jeremiah 29:11 that tells us God has a plan for us that is not orchestrated to harm us but rather to give us hope and a future. This promise is powerful and quoted by many Christians, but let me provide you with insight into the principle here.

In the previous verses of Jeremiah 29, you see that the Israelites were in captivity for 70 years and sought a word for their future. God told them not to be deceived by any false prophets or diviners because He did not send them. Instead, God told them directly His word: the allotted 70 years were reached for disobedience. He would take them back to their homeland and restore them.

This verse, verse 11, then is God's promise that although He allowed them to be captured and enslaved, His promises to them were not cut off. The time held in captivity should have given them a new and better perspective towards Him and hopefully developed a posture of obedience.

Therefore we too are to understand the trial is only for a season. God uses it to teach, mold, and refine us so that when we reach the end of the season, we will be ready not just to live but live in the promise God made to us.

Can I tell you that the mere fact God is still allowing us to face prepared trials means that God is making sure we are ready to receive our promises? This should make us hopeful because it tells us that our future is what God is directing our process towards. Each trial is precisely focused on a flaw in us that needs correction or maturity.

We stated that the devil precisely focuses his traps on our desires and weaknesses. How much more precise is God going to be in concentrating our trials?

Our trials are molded by our weaknesses and immaturity and are exclusive to our maturation. You see, desires are not wrong, but if not managed and controlled, we allow a good or natural desire to become a tool of destruction.

Our trials are molded by our weaknesses and immaturity and are exclusive to our maturation.

HAVE PATIENCE

To be patient can be one of the most challenging things anyone can ask you to do when you are drowning in distress and frustrations. But patience is precisely what God is expecting from us. Rationally, in the flesh, we may wonder if God understands what He is asking of us. Being patient during trying circumstances is not exactly a walk in the park on a Sunday afternoon after a nice family lunch. In reality, we are being challenged to transcend our rational thinking and quiet every concern of the flesh. We also have to negate what our eyes, ears, and emotions tell us and trust in Him just like a sheep does to its shepherd *(Psalms 23)*. Earlier we read Isaiah 40:31, and this is where and when it is to be applied.

We have no sensible choice but to wait on God because He is the only one who knows the accurate methods to apply to get the perfect outcome. Imagine being in a burning building with a fireman instructing you to wait until he can help you to safety. Instead of relying on the fireman's judgment, imagine yourself eyeing a window across the room that you believe you can climb through to safety. You are tempted to make a run for it before the flames reach you. You see the window as your last chance for escape to safety despite the fireman's advice.

This is precisely what can happen during your trials: you want to react based on your logic and senses and make the move that seems right to you. In the burning building, you are just waiting for the opportunity to run to the window and climb out to safety. But wait! Unknown to you, there is some critical information that you are missing. The fireman has instructed you to wait because the floor has weakened due to the fire below. Unbeknownst to you, anywhere you step could cause you to plunge through the burning floor below into a blazing fire. Even the floorboards next to the window have already weakened. The fireman is also aware that an escape through that window leads to a dangerous drop that is likely to kill you. And even if you reach the window and decide not to jump, you will be trapped in an even more dangerous position than your present one.

Like the fireman in that scenario, the Holy Spirit is our help, and He knows the safe and best steps to take. Unless we wait on Him, we might quickly run to the window of opportunity, jump through it and dive straight to a disastrous outcome (if we manage to make it to the window).

With no patience, you get no guidance, and with no guidance, you get no true success.

FAITHFUL IN PRAYER

We all know what prayer is and the importance of prayer, having discussed it earlier, but do we understand the need for *"Continual Prayer"*? We constantly hear that prayer changes things. I want to take it a bit further and say, *"Prayer changes our attitude of self-sufficiency to that of humility, which sets the stage for God to work on our behalf."* Once God steps in, we know that there will always be a great outcome. Within our trials, we can engage in many types of prayers: prayers of distress, repentance, surrender and humility, guidance, thankfulness, and many more.

In I Thessalonians 4:16-8, Paul urges us to *"Be joyful always; pray continually; give thanks in all circumstances, for it is the will of God for your lives."*

Having a thankful heart in prayer does so much for our spirit! Since prayer is communication and agreement with God, we should always stay in contact and keep the lines of communication open. Even in work situations, any successful and effective employee must be aware of what is required of him by the boss. Especially if his line of work brings new events and situations regularly.

Let's take an example from American football. The quarterback is the main player on the offensive line and has to call or set up the plays for his team to win the game. Although he may have been at all the practices and team meetings, he still wears a headphone and microphone in his helmet that keeps him in constant contact with his coach during the game.

This way, the Coach can constantly relay plays and strategies to execute while the game progresses. Anytime the microphone malfunctions and loses contact, he is at a loss to the coach's commands, expectations, and tactical advice. He cannot receive essential guidance and is very vulnerable to mistakes and failure. It is not that the quarterback is clueless about how to play the game. Rather, the coach's vantage point from the sideline enables him to spot the opposing team's formation and quickly call a play to counter the opposition's strategy. I recently learned that there could be as many as 40-50 plays which the quarterback must learn effectively to be able to respond quickly if the coach calls anyone of them. Likewise, we may study and learn the Word and acquire knowledge, but when life's curves are thrown at you, and you have to make a quick counter-attack, the knowledge must be strategically applied. In these moments, this is when your Head Coach, the Holy Spirit, instructs you on the best "play" to implement. The "play" that will bring victory! Unless you are in constant communication, how can you hear and know what play to run?

You may be thinking that the head coach is doing all the talking, and all you need to do is listen, but our listening must be constant, and the channel must be open. You also have to be familiar enough with your coach's voice to pick it up even amidst loud background noises or distractions *in your surroundings.*

Prayer not only allows you to talk to God but also helps keep your channel of communication clear and free from all distractions. Most of all, prayer helps you to remain confident in your relationship with Him. Like the confident quarterback on the field, we will have that level of confidence because we are in tune with God, and our spirits are built up and affirmed.

With the Holy Spirit as our coach, we can be sure that *"we are conquerors through Christ Jesus who loves us and neither death nor life; neither angels nor demons; neither the present nor the future; nor any powers; neither height nor depth; nor anything else in all creation, will be able to separate us from the love of God."* (**Romans 8: 38-39)** And to cap it all off, *"no weapon [or trap] that the enemy brings to us can overcome us." (**Isaiah 54:17**)*

13

WALK IN YOUR IDENTITY

There are too many Christians living a defeated and sorrowful life. How can we expect to impact, change and save lost souls if we are acting like we are the ones that need saving from our stressful lives? Would you ask a beggar for money or a homeless person for a place to live? These are the type of questions that the unbelievers have because of the poor Christian lifestyles they see exhibited daily. We are the righteousness of God, and if you are not clear on what it means, you need to pay close attention to this chapter.

Jesus suffered abuse, disgrace, pain, and ultimately, death so that everyone who calls on His name and seeks forgiveness from their sins will receive salvation. Not just salvation from eternal death but salvation (Shalom) from all measures of bondage that the devil, through this world system, has put on us.

Salvation allowed us to be victors over the devil in all areas of life. It allowed us to be free from guilt and shame due to anything we ever did in our past. It allowed us to have authority over anything on this earth that takes us to predestined purpose in God and ultimately our Sonship. And one of my favorites, salvation also allowed us total forgiveness for sins that we may fall into in the future. Why? Because our sins are no longer a bother to the devil but are nailed dead to the cross with Jesus. *We are **MORE** than conquerors.*

Because of such a free and expensive gift that we are given through simple faith and acceptance, Jesus empowers us to be the "The head and not the tail" in this "World System." A system that is solely designed to imprison and strangle anyone or anything that is for God and His purpose. The World System is wired to keep individuals bound, lost, confused, and distracted from the real meaning of life. We are called to serve and praise Jesus Christ while being reformed to the likeness of His Son to become God's Sons.

What I've learned is we are born to succeed because God has deposited all that we need to succeed in us. However, we are wired to fail because of our thinking that is continually warring against God and His ways. So although the plan is a success, our wired-to-fail and self-destructive mindset will always prevail until we have something done with our thinking. Proverbs 23:7 tells us what we think in our heart; we will live out. Hence, faulty thinking leads to bad outcomes, which leads to failure.

Suppose we have faulty thinking, and that produces our actions of life. In that case, it will also be influential in our identity and how we see ourselves. Don't think for one moment that you can have a wrong mindset and not have an identity crisis. When Adam and Eve disobeyed, we also saw that they no longer knew how to relate to God. If they don't know what their creator is thinking about them, how can they know what to think about themselves?

Flawed mindsets lead to insecurity and low self-esteem. Low self-esteem then manifests in recoiling from persons due to fears, and then we begin living out those fears.

CALLED TO GOVERN

Have you ever read of Jesus complaining in the Bible? Not even when Christ was on His journey of death was He even complaining or disgruntle. So why do we find it so necessary to complain at every trial life throws us? Why do we behave like victims rather than victors who can do all things through Jesus Christ, who strengthens us? We should not apologize for being what God created us to be (governors), nor do we have to be timid of declaring it.

We are to govern the earth in every area of life, but the devil has cleverly twisted the perspective of Christianity and its true identity. To declare that we are governors or simply heads, we have first to say, "In Jesus, I am…" We do not have to be apologetic for being kings in and of this world.

Psalms 8 vs. 6 tells us we were made governors over the works of God, and if the Bible is true as we know it to be, then we (God's sons) are to govern our Father's business. I know it sounds bold to say Christians reign over all the earth because many people, especially Christians, strongly believe that you need to be humble and poor to serve God faithfully. That is one of the most significant lies the enemy has fed humanity and has poisoned the Christians' minds against money and all that goes with it. If you don't believe me, try to effectively operate a business, ministry, or institution for God without a good cash flow and see how much you can do.

A Christian's priority is not and should never be the money, but the money is needed to fuel the ministry. The devil has attached "The love of money is the root of all evil (1 Timothy 6 vs. 10)" and "… It is easier for a camel to go through the eye of a needle than for a rich man to enter the Kingdom of God (Matthew 19 vs. 24) to the lie of Christians not needing money. These scriptures foster a mentality that once a Christian or any person possesses money, they will be corrupted by the money or will not serve God. The money will automatically become their God. It is not the possession of money that is the problem but rather the value placed on it. Money should be seen as one thing and one thing alone, a vehicle that's fueled by the purpose of God for your life.

Money only magnifies the true person of the individual.

Christians need to understand that ruling on earth goes along with the title of being a Son of God and not just worship. The key to ruling is serving humbly and obediently. A quality a Christian must possess is humility.

In John 13 we see an account where Jesu decided to create a teachable moment by washing the feet of His Disciples. Peter realizing this jumped up and told Jesus he would not allow Him to wash his feet. Peter in all honesty was seeing Christ as the Lord and instead he should be washing Jesus's feet. But Jesus said to Him "..*if I do not wash your feet you are not part of Me.*" Jesus then explanation explained to them that if He's humble enough to wash His

Disciples' feet then they should never be too proud to wash one another's feet because the servant is never greater than the Master and if the Master humbled Himself to serve then they must do the same.

Jesus taught the Disciples, us, a very important and essential principle that we need to learn and live. We are here to serve and to serve mean we must be humble because is what qualifies you for God's favor and the lack of humility will cause God to reject you.(James 4:6)

The more we humble ourselves before God through worship and service, the more He uses us to govern and steward His work. James 4 vs. 10 tells us, *"Humble yourself before the Lord, and He will raise you up in due time."* His time. We all must go through the process of refinement in humility, which has to be a choice. Once we humble ourselves, God teaches us how to serve Him with our lives and raises us to govern in our due season. Take a look at any of the true life-changing evangelists around the world and their history and see if they did not spend their time in the "Boiling Pot of Humility."

God demands us to obey! Deuteronomy 11vs.13-14, *"So if you faithfully obey the commands I am giving you today- to love the Lord your God and serve Him with all your heart and with all your soul-(14) then I will send rain(blessings) on your land (life) in due season…"* We cannot want a better command than this! We were created to serve God in sacrificial praises and worship. As we fulfill this purpose, God gives us divine authority that is manifested in the earth.

Everything physical always has a spiritual parallel.

Be aware that heavenly principles govern earthly life. We need to know or remember that we live according to the seasons and allowance of God. A basic act of sowing in expectation of reaping produce is earthly, but it is the foundational spiritual principle used to govern life. ("…A man reaps what he sows." Galatians 6 vs. 6) Whatever you want in life, you must sow first. You want love, you must express love. You want respect, you must first respect others. You want money, you must first give money. This principle is also foundational for the negative. It is no secret; whatever you sow into the ground of life, you will reap.

Whatever we sow, the nurturer of life is TIME, and you can be guaranteed that it will mature whatever you plant and give you back a harvest. We often want a harvest and don't plant anything, or we plant one thing and expect a harvest in something else.

Before, if we had said that the world teaches us to hoard everything and seek to get forward in any way, that would not be true. Being that the devil is the master of counterfeits, he has copied this principle in the world system and uses it very successfully. Look at Microsoft, for example. They are one of the wealthiest corporations in the world and the largest monetary donors in the world. Now it gets better! Bill Gates is now considered one of the richest men in the world, valued at over 128 billion dollars. Need I say more? Don't you think the devil will use anything to keep a soul in his corner? Suppose it seems that he is offering the same thing Christianity does, just better because of the supposedly flamboyant additives. In that case, it makes it harder for someone to walk away.

God wants us to realize our true identity in Him that we received when we were saved. We were given freedom from sin and all its bondage, given victory in every situation, even before we encountered them, and given authority over everything to use to accomplish our calling. This was all made possible through Jesus' death and resurrection. Either we receive the total package of salvation (Freedom, Victory, and Authority), believe and walk in it, or slap Jesus in the face by saying all that He did was in vain and only accept a part. God does not do in part, nor does Salvation come in part! We need to receive what it means to be called *"Sons of God, Heirs to the Heavenly Throne, Brothers to the Lamb of Life, and Reflections of God being used to fulfill His purpose and to pour out His glory on earth."* Jesus ruled on earth while serving God in purpose and carried out all that His Father called Him to do.

I am not telling you to walk around proud like you are above all because God hates a proud heart. I am telling you, though, to be affirmed in who you are, be humble before God and man, and walk in the full authority that God gave you. God called you, and you answered the call, so wear His name with honor.

You are a reflection of God and whatever revelation you have of God is what you will walk in, and others are going to believe Him to be that for their lives. Either He brings total happiness and fullness in your life, or He makes you miserable and complacent. Which identity of God are you portraying?

14

AN ATTITUDE OF ANTICIPATION

To be able to believe in your heart and say with conviction that God is your Father should stir up real pride and joy in your spirit that leaves you with a sweet sense of peace and security. God does not orchestrate your trials to prove to Him that you are tough and capable. Instead, they are orchestrated for you to understand the power vested in you through the acceptance of Jesus Christ. You are cloaked in His Righteousness and must be prepared to walk in it. God's righteousness brings an attitude of expectation and anticipation of Him to change situations in our favor miraculously. We must expect God's mighty hand to always move on our behalf *(Isaiah 66.vs.9)*. How else can you believe Romans 8:28 when it tells us all things will work out for God's children? Favor and miracles have to occur!

While we face the trials life has for us, we must be prepared and always joyous. 1 Thessalonians 5:18 instructs us to *"Give thanks in all situations because it is the will of Jesus Christ in us."* Why? God is working on our behalf, and He is neither weak nor incompetent. *"God is able to do above all that you could ever ask or imagine..."(Ephesians 3:20).* This verse is popular, but while we only hear this part, there is more that says, *"...According to His power that is at work within us."* Keep in mind that:

1: *The Lord can only work through us as much as we allow Him.*

2: *His power is only as effective in us as we believe.*

3: *What we believe and anticipate is what we will receive.*

We must first believe God will do exactly what He says and NEVER let the situation determine our expectations. Despite what it looks like, God will work it out according to what is best for us. The Lord is not sending Jesus again to do more miracles and save more lives. That is what we are here to do through Christ, who equips us. We are the ones to do the miracles. We are the ones to lead the lost to Christ. We are the ones to show the world what it means to be the Sons of God.

If we believe God is God and is everything we could ever want, then we must live it, walk in it, and continually declare it. Many times we have to declare the Word continually until we eradicate the old mentality. If you do not have an attitude of Expectation and Anticipation, then *receive it* and *declare it* every morning. Do this until your spirit *feels it,* which signifies you now *believe it*. Only when you live in the posture God created for you will you be able to receive all He prepared for you. If you believe the Word when it tells you God wants you to prosper in all areas of your life, then you must act like it. God is neither a liar nor a prankster!

15

OVERCOMING TRIALS

When God gives us commands, we need to be obedient and follow them precisely!

Accept that our earthly knowledge is very limited. God gives us directions that will keep us safe even though they may look cloudy and impossible to us. *"The Lord is our Shepherd....He leads us in paths of righteousness for His namesake..."* (Psalms 23:1,3).

Walk in your righteousness!

Have childlike faith that believes in the abilities and capabilities of your Father to take care of you. The even greater comfort and reassurance come in knowing that God is always at your side throughout the trials.

A young child depends entirely on his parents because he knows they will always protect and care for him. Do you entirely trust your Heavenly Father? If so, act like a child who walks honorably and takes pleasure in stating who his dad is. Walk in your identity of *Child of the Greatest Dad*.

Accept that God has a purpose for each trial!

Each trial we encounter is critical to the development of our character and helps develop awareness in some area of our life that needs to be strengthened. Each trial helps bring us to the state of wholeness God desires for us. God knows our strengths and weaknesses, and even more so, knows our capacity for life's trials.

By staying grounded in Him, we can endure all things. As a branch connects to the tree and all of its characteristics are replicas of the tree, we are connected to God. Our systems and characteristics should be like His. The keys to success at this stage are maintaining the connection to God and walking according to His daily revelations.

16

RECEIVING YOUR PROMISES

You must get to know God and understand His culture! Knowing God is much more than hearing about Him or feeling close to Him. To know God is to learn His heart towards us, which speaks to our relationship with Him. To understand His culture is to learn and apply His principles. These principles, when practiced, release the blessings and success of the Kingdom in our lives. This lifestyle is only possible through accepting Him as Lord of your life, honest and devoted time in His Word, and continual prayer.

Knowing God gives us positioning to access the blessings of being a child and joint-heir to the Kingdom, but we have as much authority as a slave. We are then given a tutor to teach us the principles of the Kingdom. At the appointed time of maturation, the Father can then declare our Sonship and confer on us the authority to operate and function in the King's name.

What I am saying is that as long as an heir is underage, he is no different from a slave, although he owns the whole estate.² The heir is subject to guardians and trustees until the time set by his father. – Galatians 4:1-2

This authority is only given to a Son who qualifies after being schooled and equipped by the tutor and considered mature. To be a Son of God speaks to maturity and is synonymous with authority. To operate in this authority is what then allows you to live out what Jesus taught in the Lord's prayer when

He said, *"Thy Kingdom come, Thy will be done."* You cannot do the will of the Father unless the authority to do so has been conferred upon you.

If you understand that, then you can understand why God opened the heavens and declared, *"this is My Son in whom I'm well pleased."* You can understand that God was saying that Jesus was now matured and ready to execute the call on His life with the authority and power conferred on Him through the Holy Spirit. God did not give Jesus the authority because He was Immanuel, but because He had learned the principles as a human and understood the Father's expectations.

Understanding the Father meant He also understood the Father's expectations of Him. Most of all, He understood the mandate and vision of the Kingdom.

As you feed on God's Word, practice a good prayer life, and submit to the refinement of the Holy Spirit, your mind is renewed. You must allow His Word to be your blueprint for living and the Holy Spirit to be the in-the-moment guide that empowers you to do all you've been assigned to do. This serves to transform you, and once this process begins, your walk with God becomes much more passionate and purposeful. You become more authoritative, victorious, and free from your old bondages and hindrances. Your core values will reflect honesty and integrity, and you will become a positive person. Your first instinct will be faithfulness to God as you honor His calling for your life. You will be granted favor by all persons and will achieve prosperity in all areas.

Without Him, we can do nothing worthwhile or achieve nothing [*John 15 vs. 5, "I am the vine; you are the branches. If you remain in me and I in you, you will bear much fruit; apart from me you can do nothing.* Accepting and understanding our need for God is the very first step to make if we are to conquer the trials and overcome the traps. It is not enough to be nominal Christians. We have to rely on God's precise guidance in each situation, made available through timely revelations.

We cannot make it without wisdom, and wisdom comes from God. So ultimately, if we are to walk in success, we need to know God personally and intimately to draw from that wisdom.

Once you know Him, apply His ways and live by His principles. No trap will hold you, and no trial will be unconquerable. Mistakes will happen but seek repentance, realign yourself, and continue walking in God's grace. God honors everything we do in and for His name out of our love for Him.

When the trials become tough and life seems too much to bear, remember God is by your side, working steadily on your behalf to ensure that you will always be successful. Because of your faithfulness to Him, He will always be faithful to you.

Trust in God's principles and ways, apply them in ultimate faith to everything in your life, and rely on His revealed wisdom each day in every trial. He will guide you to victorious living. Don't let the enemy trick and trap you while you are in your process of refinement and maturation. Stay close to God, constantly communicate with Him in prayer, listen obediently to the Holy Spirit and live in the Spirit to discern all the traps set daily. Always invoke the Kingdom of God in all situations.

The devil is only as powerful as you allow him to be in your life. Despite all the schemes and tricks that I have uncovered in this book, he has one basic plan: exploit your weaknesses and make you feel inadequate and unworthy.

Don't become so proud that you think you have overcome your weaknesses for all time, because as the familiar **Proverbs 11: 2** says, "*pride is the gateway for all destruction.*

Don't ever be caught unaware, as the devil will return again and again and again. But do not let him be a problem. As long as you keep your focus on the Kingdom of God, you will continually overcome.

You will have to go through trials as a Christian, but you do not have to be trapped, embarrassed, and cast down. These are just lies of the enemy. And if nothing else that I have said in this book stays with you, let this small piece of advice remain:

Never accept that you are supposed to be poor, defeated, and always burdened and stressed! Christ died for your total freedom and wholeness, and if He endured such pain, disgrace, and inhumane treatment, why should you relive it again?

When Psalms 23:4 says, *"...Even though I walk through the valley of the shadow of death...."* it literally means what it says. Christ walked through the very door of death. What we are walking through in this life is only a shadow of what Christ went through.

Trials are God's personally catered encounters focused on the maturation that will equip us to receive the authority to accomplish our assignment. Don't let the devil's traps derail or slow you down. Let God be able to say to the devil, "Have you considered my Son" because God knows that no matter what trap is schemed and set, you will not fall into it. God knows that you understand that man shall not live to satisfy his desires alone but to live on every word and command that gives life.

No trap is too big, too strong, or too cleverly schemed that you need to be tricked and trapped. Stay Alert and Live Triumphantly! It is your inheritance.

Before you close this book, let me just pray and declare God's plans and purpose over your life.

Most kind and precious Father, we thank you for always being on the job for our lives. I pray for the person reading this book right now that it would resonate deep in their spirit and bring forth life. I declare it will bring clarity and revelation to them, and the principles outlined here will equip and empower them not just to survive their trials but excel, mature and prosper through them.

Hosea 4:6 tells us, *"your people perish because they lack vision & revelation..."* and so, I curse the spirit of ignorance over every life that's reading this book. They will be fruitful and multiply as you intend because they have revelation and this revelation brings light to their life.

Lord, let this time spent reading this book be an investment into their future and bring such a stir in their spirit that they will be doers and not just hearers.

Bless them, Lord! Honor their desires, and most of all, let them know by your Holy Spirit that you are always right there. As the Psalmist David encourages us, you are always right there and providing all we need to succeed no matter where we find ourselves. Even when they mess up and find themselves in hell-like situations Lord, we thank you that You are still there hovering and never leaving us to die in our state.

I speak endurance and perseverance to their spirits, Lord. I speak power to their souls. I speak life to their dry bones and declare that they will fulfill the purpose you created them for and that they will becomes Sons and Daughters of You.

I declare that they will count it a joy as they go through every trial that produces maturity and will not be trapped due to their uncontrolled desires. I declare they will be vigilant and not tolerate the devil's conversations that lead to their demise.

I speak life, Lord. Life to every area of their lives, and as they receive, they will go and deposit into the creation that is eagerly awaiting their arrival.

Thank you for doing it now, Lord. I ask and declare these things in no other name but in the powerful and precious name of Jesus Christ, and for His sake, Amen!

Printed in the United States
by Baker & Taylor Publisher Services